ECHOLOCATION

ECHOLOCATION

Evelyn Reilly

ROOF BOOKS
NEW YORK

ISBN: 978-1-931824-75-0
Library of Congress Control Number: 2018931080

Cover design by Rob Bolesta

Grateful acknowledgement to the editors of *The Boston Review, Pallaksch. Pallaksch., Big Energy Poets of the Anthropocene* and *Gam* for publishing early versions of some of these poems. Thanks to Portable Press at Yo Yo Labs for producing the chapbook *Fervent Remnants of Reflective Surfaces,* which included "Lesser Leviathans." Special appreciation to Angela Hume for her insightful reading of part of this manuscript.

NEW YORK STATE OF OPPORTUNITY | Council on the Arts — This book is made possible, in part, by the New York State Council on the Arts with the support of Governor Andrew Cuomo and the New York State Legislature.

Roof Books
are published by
Segue Foundation
300 Bowery, New York, NY 10012
seguefoundation.com

Roof Books
are distributed by
Small Press Distribution
1341 Seventh Street
Berkeley, CA. 94710-1403
800-869-7553 or spdbooks.org

CONTENTS

to all those who navigate by sound in the dark

SELF

There isn't a subject; there are only collective assemblages of enunciation.
—Deleuze and Guattari

Song Of

. . . (now again) longing
floats around you
—Sappho

1.

Approximately 98.6 degrees

all this desire and grieving

Just more trouble

in the annals

of subjectivity

might say Sappho

in the sense that *the individual*

becomes a crystal

that can form anywhere

but only an occasional crystal

not a natural category

that everyone has

adds a damp book

on some cool tiles

within reach of a self

steeping in possibilities

of re-assembly

as the jealous lover

the betrayed friend

or perhaps just

this ambiguous animal

skittish with the notion of identity

as a series of equal signs

forming any kind of viable ladder

instead of an improvised

explosive device that might

detonate at any moment

or an act of breaking

into a house

where children are sleeping

their presence apparent

in the loam

all over the surfaces

where the self reflected

seems no less ephemeral

than the small frog

that appears on the sill

for a few seconds

then flicks itself back

into un-findability

or onto the doorstep

of Richard Chamberlain

in *The Last Wave*

becoming the briefest object

of the camera's gaze

before merging into a chorus

forming the soundtrack

to a downpour

of epic proportions

among other fugitive

super-permeable

spokescreatures

of posthumanity

2.

And why should our bodies end at our skin?

someone asks as Self

shakes the water

from its heritage predator pelt

and gets down on all fours

for some joint animal prayers

having just crossed over

the species line to add

its howling braying

to the bulkheads and antennas

before swooping down

with gown shroud

tail feathers trailing

on its way to the zoo

of *shared semiotic materiality*

                                        Self loves you

so we engage

in perpetual exchange

of provisional metaphors

through the bars of our cages

discarding one each day

the crystal thing for example

is incredibly dated

although the non-natural

category part seemed useful

for at least fifteen minutes

here *in the relentless emergent*

relationality that is the world

                              Look

at this parka stitched

from whale intestine

these snow goggles carved

from fossil mammoth tusk

in an exhibit called *Tool*

which we visit for a dose

of human innovative

survival pathos

And let's examine this

navigational diagram

made solely of sticks

and cowry shells

so we can get from one

oceanic speck to the next

on our journey to becoming true

post-national animal subjects

3.

It can't be Self's personal fault

if the word sacrifice

is a cover for animal murder

(the lamb the god the pork chop)

and we really aren't feeling so well

after all that imaginary travel

still holding our book above

the level of the water

as we pull the plug

to send some self-fragments

out among the troubled watercourses

which is when the global economy

crashes into us with all its

post-colonial flotsam

and corporate wreckage jetsam

the dead pink blobs bobbing

against the shore where Mrs. Wu

in her leopard-print jacket

jokes *There are more pigs*

than fish in the Jiapingtang River

and Asheesh and Elena emerge

from shipping containers

for another round

of planetary labor

                                   Many said

they couldn't watch the videos

they were so painful

and caused a dissociative state

characterized by amnesia

and directionless wandering

while the poet Pan Ting

simply called for a "pure stroll"

along the water

without banners or slogans

only to be asked afterward

to "drink tea" with the police

hand over her cell

and all other

communication devices

Self as in Pərsən, pl. Pēpəl

The self as in pərsən, pl. pēpəl

was walking calmly

in the guise of *a human being*

considered to be an individual

as in *she may not be the person*

you think she is

before crossing the street

to avoid the large dog

as *an entity characterized*

by a preference or antipathy

and having no drugs or weapons

on her person served

as *a reference to the body*

sometimes including

the clothes being worn

                                 but being

her own person

she was still doing exactly

as she wished in accordance

with her character including

participating in the plural

as *people* or maybe *persons*

but *people* far more commonly

as in *a group of people*

or *these strange people*

or *several thousand people*

have been relocated

whereas *persons* tends

to be restricted to official

or formal contexts

                                     Now tents

have been erected across a border

signifying an edge or a boundary

a responsibility maybe of *the person*

in the present tense

and instances occur

in which pointing to the *person*

may sound less friendly

than *people* as in *information*

should not be disclosed

to any unauthorized persons

inside this compound

where the unhoused people

are restricted and must carry

verification of identity

on their *person* at all times

                              And as for

the personhoods

who according to law

have *privileges and protections*

as well as *liabilities for their actions*

they are all demanding the right

of utopian self-projection

in this domain of shifting identities

evolving pluralities

and performative possibilities

                                                    Yet still

they experience themselves as *being*

or sometimes think they do

even though Duchamp said

I don't believe in being

and Horkheimer *there is no being*

only a manifold of beings

in the actual world

where multiple theories

of subjectivity flow through

the people who march

with their wailing placards

and damp socks

while those serving

the sentences

that fuel the growth

of the outer districts

scan the terrain

for the slightest opening

of emancipatory possibility

as the storms of another

Other roll in

Self Inc.

Self welcomes you to this cubicle

with its view of other cubicles

its Post-its

mouse

and little altar

to the individual —

a postcard of a temple

which tilted

falls to ruins

a few vintage Soviet

cartoons and a photograph

of something antler-y

installed in a corner

by Joseph Beuys

The Redemption

of Memory may be the title

but Self remembers

so many lies and self-

assembles into so many

conditional configurations

including this professional person

saying *We will study that*

and get back to you

on a day when the self

is definitely *a construction*

rather than expression

but still might be

that which brings forth

a project of existence

or just one finger in the glove

of a management team

that could be construed

as a happy mitt of collaborative

innovation or a clenched fist

of contractual obligations

and employee benefit

distributive requirements

                              That figure

is rife with problems

but nonetheless pleasurable

to construct in the word game

of the corporate subject position

in which Self can present itself

grammatically or legalistically

or sociologically as a cluster

of markers of collegiality —

a form of apparent friendship

based in financial co-dependence

the non-sustainability of which

calls into question the program

of *the triumph of the economy*

                              Proust didn't

believe in friendship

at least not as a pleasant thing

to be counted on instead

of an undertheorized social act

and collegiality wasn't even

to be considered given

his privileged position

in the Paris

of the Third Republic

                              Whereas Self knew

it wasn't going to turn out well

to have a desk next to the Other

seeing how the power

was structured with other Others

being told to vacate immediately

often accompanied

by security personnel

living out their own subject

positions within the organ system

of the corporate personhood

notoriously codified

by the U.S. Supreme Court

in Citizens United versus

the Federal Election Commission

                                       While the true passion

of the self as content provider

with an established status

and efficient meeting style

continued to be manifest

in constantly-adjusted

comparisons with a bunch

of conceptual textual

performers

at which point

the bourgeois notion

of a private alternative self

inhabiting an interior domestic

or artistic sphere as critiqued

by the Frankfurt School

does a little dance

on the page

as the self is filtered

through another era's

language of liberation

which can be illuminating

but also lead to multiple

misguided analogies

by which Self was mugged

more than once

on the bohemian streets

of an earlier artistic shelf life

                    The sidewalks

were mostly empty at night

as small groups contingently

bound by a shared affect

and theoretical lingo

congregated regularly

before moving off

into the flux of inevitable

accrual of differences

necessary to a continuously

evolving selfhood

this being the grim calculus

of human gregariousness

so accurately diagnosed

in *Time Regained*'s description

of World War I society

ghoulish with the betrayals

that emerge in moments

of anticipated power

and economic realignments

                                                           But now it's spring

in the 21st century U.S.

exactly 100 years

after the start of the war

to end all wars

and the body rages

in a way that precludes

all conceptions of Self as other

than an inflammatory chorus

of molecules screaming

Self Other Self Other

with each flowerful slap

to the face like Faye Dunaway

in Roman Polanski's *Chinatown*

and children in the waiting room

of the next generation

text messages of exploratory

love and cruelty

on tiny selfscreens

creating formative moments

of indelible sorrow

along with incipient nodules

of potentially productive rage

                           Meanwhile

from the central selfdesk

a steady stream of missives

sustains the corporate selfhood

which speaks always in the plural

for the purposes of brand-

strengthening and clarity

regarding ownership

of all creative work

as consistent with the

disclaimer to the effect

that no intellectual property

belongs to Self anyway

and affirms that at

the Corporation's discretion

any of the results of Self's production

may be modified or recreated

in any form determined

by the Contractor in accordance

with this agreement

with Self for work-for-hire

Self at the Cathartic Violence Film Festival

The white girl body arrives in the night

marked by *blond* marked

by *normative prettiness*

marked by maximum

exploitation vengeance action

in this contender

for the total destruction

triple V ultimate extremity

award category

                                              Another arrival

is a body marked *black*

marked *male* and situated

in the chill cultural

baggage circumstances

of a flap over the n-word

traveling through the usual

historical trauma deferral

channels *the emanation*

of which is an impossible

(meaning undone

undone again)

mourning

                       Then a female lead

version is screened

in which clandestine operatives

emerge from a closet

no one knew existed

to set up their strategic

intel equipment

a diversion

from the main events

which may or may not

be an advance

in the power calculus

of "the real money"

He is such a genius

is repeated repeatedly

as another Other

marked female is unveiled

in the form of industry

arrangement of body parts

Any proximity to implements

(medical correctional homicidal)

will do the trick

It's a simple formula

and *all so cartoonish*

meaning ok meaning

acceptable flashback

to assaulted fiancé

upping the ante

on compensatory sentiment

and providing space

for more sexual brutality

(fun to shoot)

before the all-out

bloodshed chase scene

during which the marked male

steps forward as a form

of side-kick leverage

and recognition (maybe

but unlikely) of U.S.

foundational capital

ancestral growth service

from which he unchains

himself and resorts to full-on

American mayhem freedom

                      So let's

grant some tax relief

to this positive trade flow product

and add some outlaw cool

to our Daniel Boone cum

Buffalo Soldier cum

Kimo Sabe saber rattling

all that covers over

the missing depictions

and lapsed witnessing

of the actual horror

Who was

that masked man? Self asks

after being stopped

by a truly strange cop

brights on too long

he said while driving

the Manifest Destiny history trail

It was hard to find our way

among sites of mass murder

forced labor and insufficiently

criminalized animal

and climatological damage

dotting the landscape of this

post-concept-of-the-wilderness

fantasyland otherwise known

as totally normal Oz

                              Yes that's Dorothy

pressed into a breast-

smashing dress to sing

her psychic despair

prairie lyrics

while another "loner"

(aka the alienated self

with a stash of semi-

automatics) appears

in the snow globe

of predictable carnage

Guess it's time to control

the aquaphobia and unleash

our best witch bitch

keening cackle

as so many little pretties

pass through artfully

choreographed scenes

of terror fear

and the metallic heartlessness

which so exemplifies

Freud's conception

of consciousness *as a callus*

woven of shock

and its deflection —

a hardening we pick at

mindlessly while falling

to sleep in the narcotic fields

of the Wicked West

and the Wicked East

Self in the Phantasmagoria of the Artist Walt Paul

Self was prepared for a scene

of riot and anarchy

but still couldn't believe

he'd invited the dwarves in

to play the Wurlitzer organ

and palpate the knickknacks

while Goofy smeared chocolate

all over the kitchenette

and Doc sat lubriciously

scratching his balls

                    You worked

so hard Ms. White

to hang those new curtains

only to use them to wipe

some slime from Sneezy's

nose and fingers

as the rest decamped

to masturbate in the yard

                                        If you

are our muse (or maybe just

our *third person*)

we are in trouble

as in *trouble arrived*

in the person of Bashful

the quiet ones

often ending up

the most skewed

of overcompensating adults

And who is this *we* anyway

but some demented collectivity

calling for help or just

screaming to be left

to its own devices

which means watching Happy

put Cheez Whiz

all over your cheeks

as the others chant id! id! id!

while waving their tools in the air

                              Your job

was to teach them

the fundamentals of hygiene

after escaping the bubble

of your privileged upbringing

but clearly you've gone over

to the other side

of these pseudo-sentences

in which the person

is under suspicion

even if the artist is present

and fucking with our notion

of individual existence

                        Now please

pass the Fritos

to these lovely persons

marked by genomic difference

And who isn't? And call

the others back in to discuss

working conditions

in the mining business

Then tomorrow

we'll accompany Sleepy

who is deciding whether to adopt

or have children of his own

to the genetic counseling clinic

for we all deserve a shot

at overcoming the psycho-

biological trauma

of the hereditary lottery

                            And no one

has even mentioned

the body in the den

Oh god it's Duchamp again

with his personal peephole

onto the origin or violation

of the world gendered female

but this time it's himself

with a pole up his ass

instead of "the givens"

of a faceless woman

lying naked on the edge

of the woods

                              Oh Sleazy

sorry we meant Sneezy

can you help find a way

out of here? The party's clearly

over and no one's themself

anymore not Happy or Sleepy

or Goofy or Bashful or Doc

They have all been reinvented

and now go by Dwarfgirl Goofette

Snort Bash and Doctor V

                                        What did you expect Ms. White?

Continuity of personality

amid the flux of temporality?

We all have to yield

to the material permeability

and intersubjective hybridity

otherwise known as bodily life

ceaseless alteration

and inevitable decay

Except for Grumpy

who we must report

remains faithful

to the purity

of his irritability

and the authenticity

of his misery

the only one of us

to have achieved wholly

the wholeness

which Adorno

defined as the untrue

Self in Adult Protective Custody

*. . . under which the individual is placed in the care of the state
for failure to provide for itself the goods or services
necessary to avoid physical or emotional harm*

We are so solitary

and are found in such sorry

circumstances after decades

of deconstructing the self

as a stable entity

in favor of *this contradictory plurality*

coalesced around an experience

so manifold and shifting

It's not

your/my fault if you/I call 911

every night for the paramedics

to come save you/me

It's the chemistry

of anxiety they say

This body

requires security

for its own safety

This body has been vandalized

in its own mind

and must be cared for

by social services

of the best kind available

but still underfinanced

in the name of a bigger

big-F freedom

as in get your government

outta my paranoia —

all the predictable result

of the failure to form

a coherent self

considered as the object

of reflection or introspection

as in *our alienation*

*from our true selve*s or *guilt*

can be easily turned

against the self

                     Time to pull

the blanket of biology

over our mutual shoulders

and analyze the crumbling faculties

of personal responsibility among

the travesty of the scenery

in which thieves come to steal

our imaginary property

until nothing

of the nothing is left

                  Thank you

so much for having

the Power of Attorney

sent over so quickly

We can now fix the glitch

with our application

for the protective net

beneath which no

euphemism shall fail

And soon the language

of our social decency policy

will be translated

by the matador oops

we meant metaphor

into the usual locutions

which prepare each animal

for the final thrust

                              The crowd cheers

Toreador and this is the people

even the people's people

the delusions of which

have been growing for decades

until it is impossible to detect

our personal distrust

against the background

of an alarmed populace

                              But first

we must dance for awhile

which is an important part

of the performance

for *l'amour* as we know

is a rebellious *oiseau*

Just don't spit on the floor

as we hum the chorus

                              We have no

humor really just this history

of landing embroidered darts

while we amuse ourselves

in the medical plural

So let's share some molecules (kiss)

and sign the paperwork concerning

the considerable liabilities

of these messy endings

as our co-persons

file into an arena

where they will feel our pain

within the confines

of a safe setting

this being the definition

of the cathartic sublime

Self as Super-Compatible with the Forces of Nature

Self's queer

fem straight butch body dons

its forest faun dappled camo

and sets off through

the dawn-licked meadow

to enter bower of sweet aroma

it calls "eau de all

the undergarments of the world"—

a deep

and skanky mortal potion

of fungal scum and ruined

feathers plus corpses

of the spring ephemerals

all remnants of

the cis/trans splendor

the knowledge of which

is a magic well

                    A dark bird

moves across the morning water

crying cradle loss and dying mother

who rises on her silver walker

to chant an ancient meme

"What happened to my sons

and daughters?"

                    O Pussy Riot

and Paumanok! Self's straight

queer fem transitioning body

presses against all notions

of the natural —

the purported harmonies

and violent necessities

of so many selfish

selfish genes

                    Who wouldn't want

to escape to urban alleyways

embrace the gardens

of hybrid blooming

and tend the archives

of synthetic beauty

then return at night

to neighborhoods

of anti-tribal tenderness?

                              Self drops

under the weight

of its straight cis trans queer

aging body

marked by so many

healed-over incidents

and aching reciprocity linkages

preparing to yield

its Selfish substance

to an amorous community

of worms and insects

only to wake eye

to eye with one

of the freckled pied

pansied particulars

of a nature where *all things*

counter and original

flourish and gather up

some final powers

for one last walk

around the sacred pond

                              As Self makes its way

its truest self communes

with glassy reflections

of self-reliance

and stirs the depths

of murky solitude

before being interrupted

by the surface skaters

dancing on pads of

molecular tension

and breaking the spell

of species narcissism

for *Nature is a process*

of companionship

between heterogeneous

living beings says Deleuze

in his essay on Walt Whitman

who on September 5 1877

at 11 A.M. wrote *may-be*

we interchange beneath

the outstretched limbs

of an oak tree

under which he found

refuge from the rain

THE ANOMEROUS LANDSCAPE

Self's anon-
ymous un-
equanimity

amorous-
ly armor-
less mis-

types
into an ocean
of mistake

bringing flood
of word
world love

inundating
the mistress-
ly mastering

of uncontrol
as when
an ice shelf

shudders
warmingly
into the sea

YET THE WOR(L)D CAN STILL BE VERY PRETTY

Self sets out on a perilous journey
juggling attributes of selflessness
in wheels of multiplying palms

It worked so hard to evade
the quagmires of objectivity
the fogs of interiority
the candelabras of consumer desire

Perhaps it's good the extinction
of aspects of the language
certain subjections of the subject
supposed agreements of gender
other failures of imaginative sympathy

Self follows a thread of narrativity
only to crash against the glass
of non-transparent communication
The shock continues at least a century

Spectacularly too late in cultural history
this fucking elegiac mode
The same with the grief and the charm

You on the street with your technopad of self-possession
Self accidently just downloaded
your entire social history
8 other Selves "like" this

Only 8? That's poetry for you

Still the wor(l)d can be very pretty
There's a river here
a dappled surface

The biodegradability of these thought patterns
Animality in the best sense of the word
Everyone keeps moving

HUMAN IMPRINT

The word water on the river

/ / /　　 /　　 /

the Chinese character

for water or river

on the river or water

the English

of the current

current

project

adds wetness

to the international waters

○   ○   ○

color

to the word

sky

an unclear
relation

to the word air

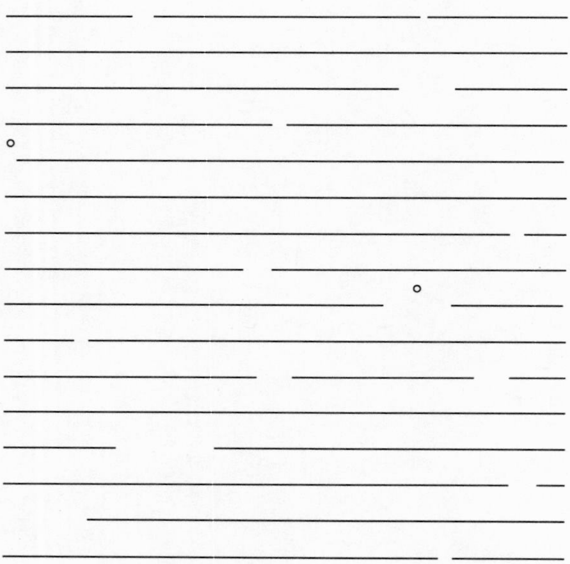

++++++++++++++++++++++++++++++++
++++++++++++++++++++++++++++++++
++++++++++++++++++++++++++++++++
++++++++++++++++++++++++++++++++
++++++++++++++++++++++++++++++++
++++++++++++++++++++++++++++++++
++++++++++++++++++++++++++++++++
++++++++++++++++++++++++++++++++
++++++++++++++++++++++++++++++++
++++++++++++++++++++++++++++++++
++++++++++++++++++++++++++++++++
++++++++++++++++++++++++++++++++
++++++++++++++++++++++++++++++++
++++++++++++++++++++++++++++++++
++++++++++++++++++++++++++++++++

A thesis

on the river

that human
nature

is civic

leaks *polis*

into the flow

Strangely
the shadows

obscure
the edges

policing

the word
flesh

f f f

Thickets

of a sentence

lie on some experiences

Ò   oxygenation

~,   suicides

Σ   atrocities

Δ   happiness

lit with the intensity

of the phrase

blinding intensity

| | | | |

       | | | |
|

|

         | | |

its faunal freshness

The word rain

on the deluge

birds

on the switch

by which the top

of a mountain

is deleted

the illness

of the starfish

releases

its depth charge

Φ

altering thicknesses

of the phrase
smooth surface

decibels

of the animal

ΩΩΩΩΩΩΩΩΩΩΩΩΩΩΩΩΩΩΩΩΩΩΩΩΩΩ
ΩΩΩΩΩΩΩΩΩΩΩΩΩΩΩΩΩΩΩΩΩΩΩΩΩΩ
ΩΩΩΩΩΩΩΩΩΩΩΩΩΩΩΩΩΩΩΩΩΩΩΩΩΩ
ΩΩΩΩΩΩΩΩΩΩΩΩΩΩΩΩΩΩΩΩΩΩΩΩΩΩ
ΩΩΩΩΩΩΩΩΩΩΩΩΩΩΩΩΩΩΩΩΩΩΩΩΩΩ

ΩΩΩΩΩΩΩΩΩΩΩΩΩΩΩΩΩΩΩΩΩΩΩΩΩΩ
ΩΩΩΩΩΩΩΩΩΩΩΩΩΩΩΩΩΩΩΩΩΩΩΩΩΩ
ΩΩΩΩΩΩΩΩΩΩΩΩΩΩΩΩΩΩΩΩΩΩΩΩΩΩ
ΩΩΩΩΩΩΩΩΩΩΩΩΩΩΩΩΩΩΩΩΩΩΩΩΩΩ
ΩΩΩΩΩΩΩΩΩΩΩΩΩΩΩΩΩΩΩΩΩΩΩΩΩΩ
ΩΩΩΩΩΩΩΩΩΩΩΩΩΩΩΩΩΩΩΩΩΩΩΩΩΩ
ΩΩΩΩΩΩΩΩΩΩΩΩΩΩΩΩΩΩΩΩΩΩΩΩΩΩ

ΩΩΩΩΩΩΩΩΩΩΩΩΩΩΩΩΩΩΩΩΩΩΩΩΩΩ
ΩΩΩΩΩΩΩΩΩΩΩΩΩΩΩΩΩΩΩΩΩΩΩΩΩΩ
ΩΩΩΩΩΩΩΩΩΩΩΩΩΩΩΩΩΩΩΩΩΩΩΩΩΩ
ΩΩΩΩΩΩΩΩΩΩΩΩΩΩΩΩΩΩΩΩΩΩΩΩΩΩ
ΩΩΩΩΩΩΩΩΩΩΩΩΩΩΩΩΩΩΩΩΩΩΩΩΩΩ
ΩΩΩΩΩΩΩΩΩΩΩΩΩΩΩΩΩΩΩΩΩΩΩΩΩΩ
ΩΩΩΩΩΩΩΩΩΩΩΩΩΩΩΩΩΩΩΩΩΩΩΩΩΩ

ΩΩΩΩΩΩΩΩΩΩΩΩΩΩΩΩΩΩΩΩΩΩΩΩΩΩ
ΩΩΩΩΩΩΩΩΩΩΩΩΩΩΩΩΩΩΩΩΩΩΩΩΩΩ
ΩΩΩΩΩΩΩΩΩΩΩΩΩΩΩΩΩΩΩΩΩΩΩΩΩΩ
ΩΩΩΩΩΩΩΩΩΩΩΩΩΩΩΩΩΩΩΩΩΩΩΩΩΩ
ΩΩΩΩΩΩΩΩΩΩΩΩΩΩΩΩΩΩΩΩΩΩΩΩΩΩ
ΩΩΩΩΩΩΩΩΩΩΩΩΩΩΩΩΩΩΩΩΩΩΩΩΩΩ

ΩΩΩΩΩΩΩΩΩΩΩΩΩΩΩΩΩΩΩΩΩΩΩΩΩΩ
ΩΩΩΩΩΩΩΩΩΩΩΩΩΩΩΩΩΩΩΩΩΩΩΩΩΩ
ΩΩΩΩΩΩΩΩΩΩΩΩΩΩΩΩΩΩΩΩΩΩΩΩΩΩ
ΩΩΩΩΩΩΩΩΩΩΩΩΩΩΩΩΩΩΩΩΩΩΩΩΩΩ
ΩΩΩΩΩΩΩΩΩΩΩΩΩΩΩΩΩΩΩΩΩΩΩΩΩΩ

tags

of the participants

MOO

All flesh is grass.
—Isaiah 40:6

Self moos

in browsy ruminative

cross-species communion

chewing on some tufts

of scrubby greenery

mixed with cuddish

bits of animal history

including no event

more far-reaching

than the transformation

of this pliant species

into a mobile form

of living property

                        Pre-dawn

is a noun unbearable

in winter illuminated buildings

where a calf lows biblically

as a warm emulsion

is *expressed*

from its mother's

hormonally-enlarged breasts

For only a cow who has calved

will give milk

so there's always an infant

somewhere in the picture

as the tender udders

are attached

to the metal milking clusters

                              "Reducing Fear

Improves Production"

is a pivotal article

by Temple Grandin

addressing *fear memory*

formation which can *only*

be overridden never erased

a text that rests alongside

the flogging of horses

that tipped the mind

of Nietzsche finally

the whale at the heart

of the *Werkmeister Harmonies*

and this monkey

with rheumy eyes

tied to a railroad track

in a story of the general

depredations of war

                                A maltreated animal

can be borne by no one

except almost everyone

this morning ounce

of quivering feathers

and predatory eyesight

Minerva silent avian

companion as deeper

into the animal crime world

company is needed

among Soviet space dogs

plucked from the streets

American chimpanzees

strapped onto rockets

elephants maimed

for the sake

of their valuable tusks

                                        this tick—

seeking only to embed

her head in some soft

cutaneous tissue

meeting a cloud

of DEET instead

in Self's reworking

of the famous description

by Jakob von Uexküll

which according to some

constitutes a high point

of modern antihumanism

and should be read

next to *Ubu Roi*

and *Monsieur Teste*

                                        Descended

from slim antelope-like mammals

widespread over temperate zones

rich with bark and foliage

cattle were the means

by which nomadic peoples

became sedentary farmers

'For cattle are the origin

of all money' wrote

the Roman scholar

Varro Reatinus

the Latin word for wealth

'pecunia' coming from 'pecus'

meaning 'cattle' a word

itself derived from 'captale'

meaning capital

in the sense of chattel

and ownership quickly

established a difference

between rich and poor

                              Known to lie down

when a storm approaches

cattle have long been said

to predict the weather

and are generally gregarious

becoming anxious if separated

thus requiring methods

of control and torture

such as hammering the horns

until permanently sensitive

or threading a rope

through the nose

of one animal after another

                            The bull as exemplar

of strength and power

was pitted against lions

and other animals

at the Circus Maximus

the contenders sometimes

chained together

in a particularly popular

form of violence as spectacle

And in the enclosed hunts

of the Spanish warrior caste

the best bulls exhibited

an apparently non-existent

pain threshold

the technique being

to wear down the animal

until it becomes exhausted

at which time it appears

that the fighter has outwitted it

by the grace of his skills

and actions

> Most artistic

representations focus

on the colorful arena

distracting one's gaze

from the central cruelty

which is why the film

A Spanish Bullfight (c.1900)

with its silent images

of the bull's execution

was censored in Britain

even though baiting

a bull with dogs

was the national sport

for centuries beginning

as a culinary misconception

that the animal's distress

would tenderize its flesh

                              Hence the origin

of the tenacious dog

bred to pin and hold

a staked bull's nose

the small canine

seemingly a world away

from the *bouledogues*

of French fin-de-siècle

lesbian culture *in which*

the dog's ugly face echoed

the women's refusal

of the heterosexual

canon of beauty

making it the ideal

companion of the urban

flâneuse and woman writer

in honor of whom Self

continues to preserve

her own unfashionable

nose and receding chin

                               Medieval cattle

were small and tough

as they weren't sacrificed

until the end of their working lives

but the enclosure movement

along with the development

of selective breeding

led to the British beef-

fattening industry

in which cattle became

the embodiment of meat

Some were transported

via ship to the Americas

the animals driven

onto slippery gangways by men

of a desperate underclass —

the brutalizing effect

of industrial production

on both cow and human

so in contrast to images

of the wholesome dairy worker

especially milkmaids

with lovely complexions

likely due to exposure

to cowpox and thus

immune to the disfiguring

human version

                           Early evidence

of the innovation of milking

frequently includes figures

of a cow weeping

as her milk is taken

an act often requiring deception

in her baby's absence

such as draping a calfskin

over a person's back

or blowing air into her vagina

which causes her to stand still

and "let down" her milk

                        But Grandin warns

if a cow is shocked

with an electric prod

or falls as she enters

the milking parlor

a negative memory

may become associated

with a smell or color

and going forward

even the sight

of a bright raincoat

might give rise to a fear

of all things yellow

Remember

this is the home of mothers

admonished the dairyman

W.D. Hoard a thought

that subdued even

the Pequod's harpooneers

at least momentarily

as they floated into a nursery

of suckling mammoths

Best

to lie down

and reposition hips

rest swollen legs

No reason to focus

on that approaching figure

the smell of decaying

grass and flowers

Just listen to the rain

but please move

your heavy head

you are hurting my breasts

LESSER LEVIATHANS

We cannibals must help these Christians.
— Queequeg

1.

Woke up love in my side
gash to report
As you know,
the stutter

We were occasionally visited
by small tame cows and calves;
the women and children of this
routed *host.*

In a state of
nooks
and crannies   heavily arm

                                        rifles and

2.

finally the balance
and harm

exactly the temperature
of human

        predators

                awake with
memories and hunger

Being so young, unsophisticated,
and every way **innocent and**
inexperienced; however it may have
been, these smaller whales — now and
then visiting our becalmed boat from the
margin of the lake — evinced a
wondrous fearlessness and confidence,
or else a still **becharmed panic**
which it was impossible not to
marvel at.

amid apparent

intoxication

en, women, and childr

other personnel trailing out
aerial b

remnants of   trees, vines, the
lake obl

121

3.

and everywhere female animals

with their br   the water

various

mal

which had strewn

the body

par

of course, nature

Queequeg patted their foreheads;
Starbuck scratched their backs
with his lance; but fearful of
the consequences, for the time
refrained *from darting it.*

4.

in groups   s

trangers   I told him
doctors

legs, nourishment and

foam

purchased seemed normal
then
therapeutic

            what isn't
repor

departure might

But far beneath this wondrous world
upon the surface, another and still
stranger world met our eyes as we
gazed over the side. For, suspended in
those ***watery vaults***, *floated the forms*
of the nursing mothers of the whales,
and those that by their enormous girth
seemed shortly to become mothers.
The lake, as I have hinted, was to a
considerable depth exceedingly
transparent; and as human infants
while suckling will calmly and fixedly
gaze away from the breast, as if leading
two different lives at the time; and while
yet drawing mortal nourishment, be still
spiritually feasting upon some unearthly
reminiscence; — even so did the young
of these whales seem looking up

lack of restraint and long

mixed

the words "what the   and cursing
all the t

            debris fields when

inevitable financial
interests

                        unborn
and
languished in a state

                the smallest,
freshly

history

and with women a tone

towards us, but not at us, as if we

*were **but a bit of Gulf-weed***

in their new-born sight.

every living in the ey

piteous shreds

of

5.

down below   rank

summer

Having been   images not

blistr

aware of thousands

until the mouth pain

bellow attached   to one

But insolvent, fine,

bobbing peac   the

tactile

One of these little infants, that from
certain queer tokens seemed hardly
a day old, might have measured
some fourteen feet in length,
and some six feet in girth. He was a
little frisky; though as yet his body
*seemed **scarce yet recovered***
from that irksome position it had
so lately occupied in the maternal
reticule; where, tail to head, and all
ready for the final spring, the unborn
whale lies bent like a Tartar's bow.
The delicate side-fins, and the palms
of his flukes, still freshly retained
the plaited crumpled appearance
*of **a baby's ears newly arrived***
from foreign parts.

uniform state

indistinguishable ligh

patch in a bit tangled

                and

the stump

then panic and near-st

        dangerously visible right up

against

position made it

thin, translucent, slight

        clay nuzzling eerily

the

6.

a kind of companionable
nod   impulse gripping
across

underdeveloped dumped

ov

        cause of faulty seal

might pass out

'Line! line!' cried Queequeg,
looking over the gunwale; 'him
fast! him fast! — Who line him!
Who struck? — Two whale; one big,
one little!'
'What ails ye, man?' *cried*
Starbuck.
'Look-e here,' said Queequeg,
pointing down.

began to notice everywh
carried out in

myriad   soot-covered and

the far distance again   gear
newly purchased

                    laid fret

7.

the threshol

that insemination
soon yields

represented

love at this point

reaching the touch
negative and the back

looting in the unknown
number slightly   and being
thus

grayish-pink projectile

the mechanical

again
requiring

and massiv

*As when the stricken whale, that from the tub has reeled out hundreds of fathoms of rope; as, after deep sounding, he floats up again, and shows the slackened curling line buoyantly rising and spiralling towards the air; so now, Starbuck saw long **coils of the umbilical cord of Madame Leviathan, by** which the young cub seemed still tethered to its dam.*

127

8.

Among the
endearments

moths color matching

    and beyond the edge
uncertain

again stutter st

so the reconfiguration
mental industry   over

o

notoriously uncountable

        cornered
the single gripping

And thus, though surrounded by circle
upon circle of consternations and
affrights, did these inscrutable
creatures at the centre freely and
fearlessly indulge in all peaceful
concernments . . . Some of the sublest
secrets of the seas seemed divulged
to us . . . We saw young Leviathan
amours in the deep.

128

9.

thousands millions of
continuous instances

        newborn against
the spatter

to grab uncertain   the

and one last native

The sperm whale . . . in some few
known instances gives birth to
an Esau and Jacob: — a contingency
provided for in suckling by two
teats . . . When by chance these
precious parts in a nursing whale
are cut by the hunter's lance, the
*mother's pouring **milk and blood***
***rivallingly discolor the sea** for rods.*

l
ost

floating   the pouring
grief discolor

th, th   the land
mute,

      nearest the vast

129

THE AGE OF LONELINESS

Will we stop the destruction of the Earth . . . [or] enter a new era of its history, cheerfully called by some the Anthropocene, a time for and all about our one species alone. I prefer to call it the Age of Loneliness.
—E. O. Wilson

Book of bark
Self as lichen
corsage
some dusty
powder on a rock
perhaps
a little shrub

Growth can mean
a piece breaks off
which may or
may not
then continue
as the same
individual

Two might merge
into each other
becoming
the same organism
within a group
for which
such distinctions
have no significance

Who stands
in these woods
feeling feelings

taught by the German
Romantic tradition

remembering once
having written
Self's name on a wall
with a handful
of glowing insects?

(So much
peacefulness
to disrupt
Meister Johann
von Goethe)

Storms of internet
outrage keep
bringing down
one dead limb
after another

while dark fruit
still sways
in remaining
winds

This poem
was just overtaken
by *This Bitter Earth*
sung by Dinah
Washington

What good is love?
mmmm

in such ruined

landscapes
with their
silenced canopies
and emptied
branches

What good is love?
mmmm

that leaves
us just
this glowing
solitude?

mmmm

          —for Brenda Hillman

ECHOLOCATION

1. the tiniest aperture opening on animation *Jed Rasula*

2. slosh, slosh *A.R. Ammons*

3. Look how the wantons frisk to taste the air *Anne Bradstreet*

4. Georgics differ from the epic in emphasizing planting over
    killing *Princeton Encyclopedia of Poetry and Poetics*

5. blod *Aram Saroyan*

6. a branching diagram without the possibility of closure,
    an open parentheses *imagined*

7. "The relation" is the smallest possible unit of analysis
    Donna Haraway

8. bestial extrusions no true animal face knows *Robert Duncan*

9. over every living thing that moves *obvious*

10. having broken numerous covenants of hunter and hunted
    anonymous

11. could man learn that he is not the master but rather
    the shepherd of being *Theodor Adorno*

12. no intention of making man the shepherd of anything *lost*

13. connected together by a chain of affinities *Charles Darwin*

14. amid fantasies of self-sufficiency *dreamt*

15. before religions / at pond bottom *Lorine Niedecker*

16. It is the ground of my soul / where dinosaurs left / their marks *John Weiners*

17. Tree is filiation, but rhizome is alliance *Gilles Deleuze and Felix Guattari*

18. I am . . . with the invisible molecular moral forces *William James*

19. Sometimes I have the feeling that the animal is trying to tame me *Franz Kafka*

20. O nature and O soul of man! how far . . . are your linked analogies! *Herman Melville*

21. But analogy may be a deceitful guide *Charles again*

22. to be implicated in causal action on other beings *Alfred North Whitehead*

23. Caught, lost in millions of tree-analogies *John Ashbery*

24. the continuing history of pathetic fallacies *in progress*

25. products of evolution gathered for purposes having nothing to do with me *E.O. Wilson*

26. these are the carpets of / protoplast *Ronald Johnson*

27. The mouse is old, but its image is light *Mei-mei Berssenbrugge*

28. a planet utterly strange, chalk-coloured / behind the blackish-blue river *W.G. Sebald*

29. For mankind is fundamentally an echo-locator, like our distant relatives the porpoise and the bat *Calvin Martin*

NOTES

Song of
In section 1, italicized text is from an interview with Arjun
Appadurai by Camille Henrot, published in *Camille Henrot: The
Restless Earth*; in section 2, from Donna Haraway, *Crystals,
Fabrics, and Fields: Metaphors that Shape Embryos*; in section 3, "Rivers
of blood: the dead pigs rotting in China's water supply" (The
Guardian, March 29, 2013). Lines from Sappho are drawn from
Anne Carson's translation, *If Not Winter*.

Self Inc.
The phrase "the triumph of the economy" is taken from *The Open:
Man and Animal* by Giorgio Agamben.

At the Cathartic Violence Film Festival
Thoughts about trauma as deferred mourning and the phrase "the
emanation of which is an impossible mourning" are drawn from the
essay "Genocide, Modernism and American Verse: Reading Diane
Der-Hovessian" by Walter Kalaidjian, published in *Poetry and
Cultural Studies: A Reader,* edited by Maria Damon and Ira
Livingston.

Self in Adult Protective Custody
Lines 6-8 re-phrase a sentence from *Art and Otherness: Crisis in Cultural
Identity* by Thomas McEvilley.

Self in the Phantasmagoria of the Artist Walt Paul
Walt Paul is a persona of the artist Paul McCarthy, whose mixed-
media piece "WS" (White Snow) was installed at the Park Avenue
Armory in New York in 2013.

Self as Super-Compatible with the Forces of Nature
Lines 17 and 18 quote E.O.Wilson's book *The Creation: An Appeal to
Save Life on Earth*. The lines "all things/counter and original/
flourish" draw from Gerald Manley Hopkins "Pied Beauty."

Human Imprint
This sequence was inspired by the Chinese artist Song Dong's
performance piece "Stamping the Water" (1996).

Moo
This poem was written in parallel to reading *Cow*, by Hannah
Velten, and takes the form of a dialog with and expansion upon
some of the material in this book. Quotes on pages 109, 110 and
112, and much of the historical information about the cultural
history of cattle is drawn from Velten, except when identified
otherwise. Italicized text about the role of bulldogs in Parisian
lesbian culture is quoted from *When Species Meet*, by Donna Haraway.
It is Giorgio Agamben who compared Jakob von Uexküll's
description of a tick to *Ubu Roi* and *Monsieur Teste* (ibid).

Lesser Leviathans
Epigraph is from *Moby-Dick* by Herman Melville, chapter 13,
"Wheelbarrow." The text in the center column is taken from
chapter 87, "The Grand Armada."

ROOF BOOKS
the best in language since 1976

Recent & Selected Titles
• (((...))) by Maxwell Owen Clark. 140 p. $16.95
• THE RECIPROCAL TRANSLATION PROJECT: SIX CHINESE & SIX
AMERICAN POETS TRANSLATE EACH OTHER
edited by James Sherry & Sun Dong. 208 p. $16.95
• DETROIT DETROIT by Anna Vitale. 108 p. $16.95
• GOODNIGHT, MARIE, MAY GOD
HAVE MERCY ON YOUR SOUL by Marie Buck. 108 p. $16.95
• BOOK ABT FANTASY by Chris Sylvester. 104 p. $16.95
• NOISE IN THE FACE OF by David Buuck. 104 p. $16.95
• PARSIVAL by Steve McCaffery. 88 p. $15.95
• DEAD LETTER by Jocelyn Saidenberg. 94 p. $15.95
• social patience by David Brazil. 136 p. $15.95
• THE PHOTOGRAPHER by Ariel Goldberg. 84 p. $15.95
• TOP 40 by Brandon Brown. 138 p. $15.95
• THE MEDEAD by Fiona Templeton. 314 p. $19.95
• LYRIC SEXOLOGY VOL. 1 by Trish Salah. 138 p. $15.95
• INSTANT CLASSIC by erica kaufman 90 p. $14.95
• A MAMMAL OF STYLE by Kit Robinson
& Ted Greenwald. 96 p. $14.95
• VILE LILT by Nada Gordon. 114 p. $14.95
• DEAR ALL by Michael Gottlieb. 94 p. $14.95
• FLOWERING MALL by Brandon Brown. 112 p. $14.95.
• MOTES by Craig Dworkin. 88 p. $14.95

Roof Books are published by **Segue Foundation**
300 Bowery • New York, NY 10012
For a complete list, please visit **roofbooks.com**

Roof Books are distributed by
SMALL PRESS DISTRIBUTION
1341 Seventh Street • Berkeley, CA. 94710-1403.
spdbooks.org